PARANORMAL TECH

Ghost Hunting with Tech

by Mae Respicio

CAPSTONE PRESS
a capstone imprint

0.0001101101
0.0001101101
0.0001101101
0.0001101101
0.0001101101

Published by Spark, an imprint of Capstone
1710 Roe Crest Drive
North Mankato, Minnesota 56003
capstonepub.com

Library of Congress Cataloging-in-Publication Data is available
on the Library of Congress website.
ISBN: 9781669049630 (hardcover)
ISBN: 9781669049593 (ebook PDF)

Summary: A shadowy figure takes shape in a dark, old house. Was it a ghost?
Ghost hunters investigate ghostly happenings with infrared cameras, EMF
meters, spirit boxes, and other gear. Get an inside look at all the high-tech tools
used to study hair-raising hauntings.

Editorial Credits
Editor: Carrie Sheely; Designer: Jaime Willems; Media Researcher: Rebekah
Hubstenberger; Production Specialist: Whitney Schaefer

Image Credits
Alamy: ZUMA Press Inc, 27; Associated Press: Edward Pevos/MLive/Ann
Arbor News, 17, Journal Gazette, Kevin Kilhoffer, 4, Stephen Brashear/
Invision for Microsoft, 11, The Fayetteville Observer, Johnny Horne, 8; Getty
Images: Barry Chin/The Boston Globe, 15, David Wall, back cover, 28, JOE
KLAMAR/AFP, 1, 5, MediaNews Group/Orange County Register, 22,
Michele Spatari/AFP, 9, Myung J. Chun/Los Angeles Times, 12; Newscom:
Joseph Kaczmarek/ZUMAPRESS, 23, Media Drum World/ZUMAPRESS, 6;
Shutterstock Premier: MY Media, 7; Shutterstock: HEakin, 25, Juiced Up
Media, front cover (meter), Nagel Photography, 18, sakkmesterke, 21,
Sensay, 16, zef art, front cover (background)

Design elements: Shutterstock: alleachday, Tex vector, zinetroN

Printed and bound in China. PO5379

Table of Contents

Words in bold are in the glossary.

Ghost Hunters

Strange shadows. Weird noises. A feeling that someone is watching you. Could a ghost be causing these eerie happenings? Ghost hunters search places said to be **haunted**. They use different kinds of technology to try to find out if ghosts are real.

Ghost hunting equipment

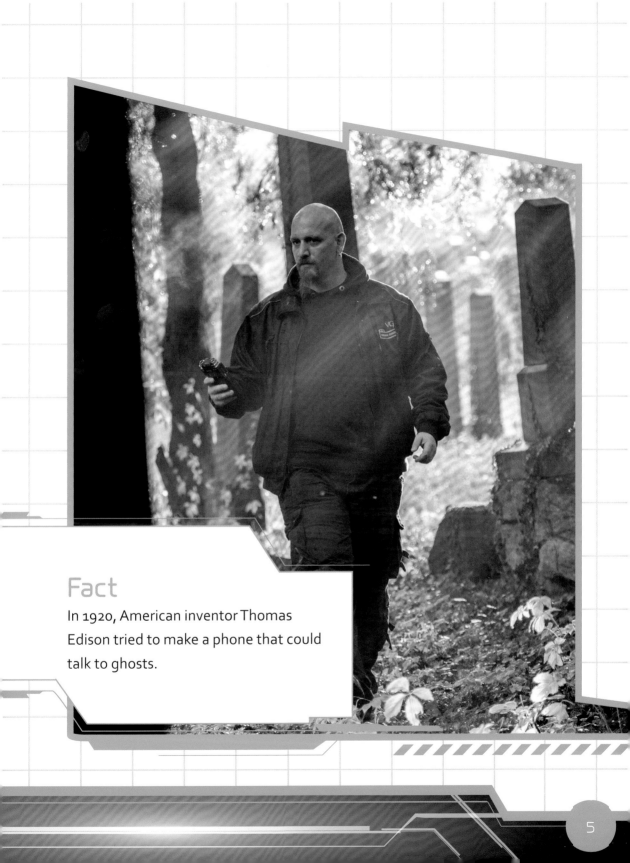

Fact

In 1920, American inventor Thomas Edison tried to make a phone that could talk to ghosts.

What Do You See?

Ghost hunters think ghosts can appear in photos. They use high-tech cameras to spot them. They look for body shapes. They look for tiny balls of floating light called **orbs**. People say ghosts can appear as orbs.

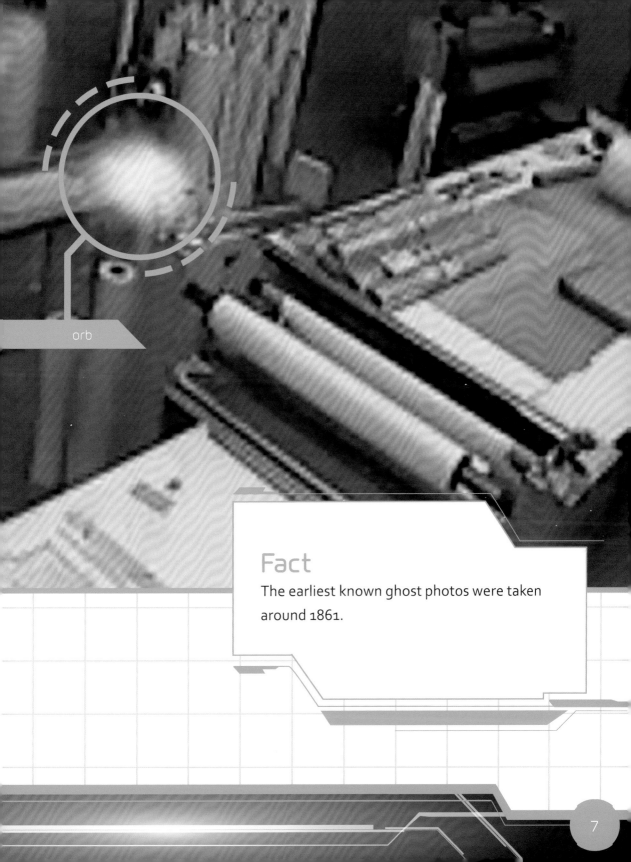

orb

Fact

The earliest known ghost photos were taken around 1861.

Infrared and thermal cameras see in the dark. They look for light that people cannot see. Thermal cameras can find cold spots. Some people say ghosts can cause cold spots.

A ghost hunter with a handheld infrared camera

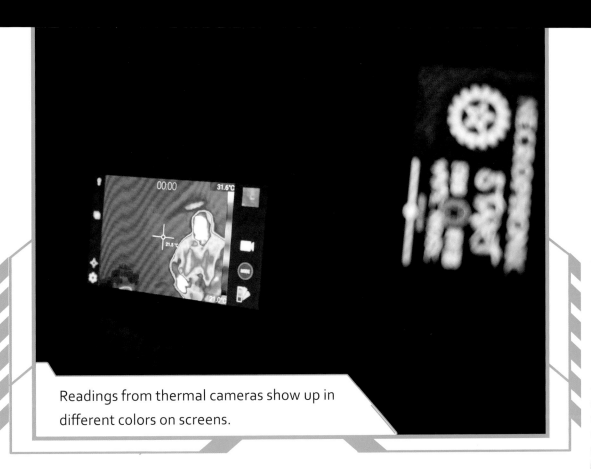

Readings from thermal cameras show up in different colors on screens.

In 2022, a woman in Massachusetts thought her house was haunted. A team used infrared cameras to find out. What happened? They saw many orbs. One orb zoomed down the stairs into the basement.

Do ghosts play video games? Maybe. Xbox once sold an add-on called Kinect. It sensed motion and tracked a player's body **joint** movement. But some people said they saw strange things. Some users said the add-on sensed other players. Yet they were the only ones playing!

Skeleton

Now, some people use Kinect to find ghosts. One ghost hunter thought she saw a small ghost child.

A ghost hunter gets an SLS camera ready to use.

SLS cameras have light sensors. Like Kinect, they sense movement. Ghosts hunters say ghosts can appear on camera screens as stick figures. One TV ghost hunting crew said their SLS camera showed a stick figure dancing.

Listen Closely

Shhhhhh! A ghost might be talking! Ghost hunters try to listen to ghosts with sound recorders. Later, they study the recordings.

A spirit box can scan radio channels. Some people say it can pick up a ghost's voice.

A ghost hunter said she once was at Eloise Asylum in Michigan. A flashlight turned on by itself. She asked the ghost to do it again. From the spirit box, she heard *da*. This word means "yes" in the Russian language. The flashlight came on.

A room inside Manteno State Hospital

Sound recordings thought to be from ghosts are called **EVP**. EVP stands for electronic voice phenomena. EVP recorders boost soft sounds. They could help a ghost's voice come through clearly.

In 2002, ghost hunters went to Manteno State Hospital in Illinois. The hospital was empty. It had no power. They walked around to record sounds. After they listened, they heard someone **paging** a doctor.

Feel the Energy

Some people set REM pods around haunted places. A pod puts out an electromagnetic field (EMF). It senses things moving into the field. If it beeps, a ghost could be near it.

People cannot see electromagnetic fields, but tools can sense them.

EMF meters track electromagnetic fields. People walk around with them. Sometimes a meter shows an EMF spike. People think this might mean it's picking up a ghost's energy.

The Morris-Jumel Mansion in New York is said to be haunted. One story says a woman inside the house yelled at kids walking by it in 1964. But no one was inside!

The mansion is now a museum. It holds haunted tours where people can use EMF meters. A meter has sensed EMFs in a bedroom.

Fact

Faulty wiring and electronic equipment can set off EMF meters. Some people say an EMF spike does not mean a ghost is near.

Ghosts Among Us

Sometimes ghosts hunters don't need to buy special tools. They can use smartphone **apps**. These include EMF meters and EVP recorders.

Ghost hunters share details of what they find online. This helps others plan where to hunt for ghosts.

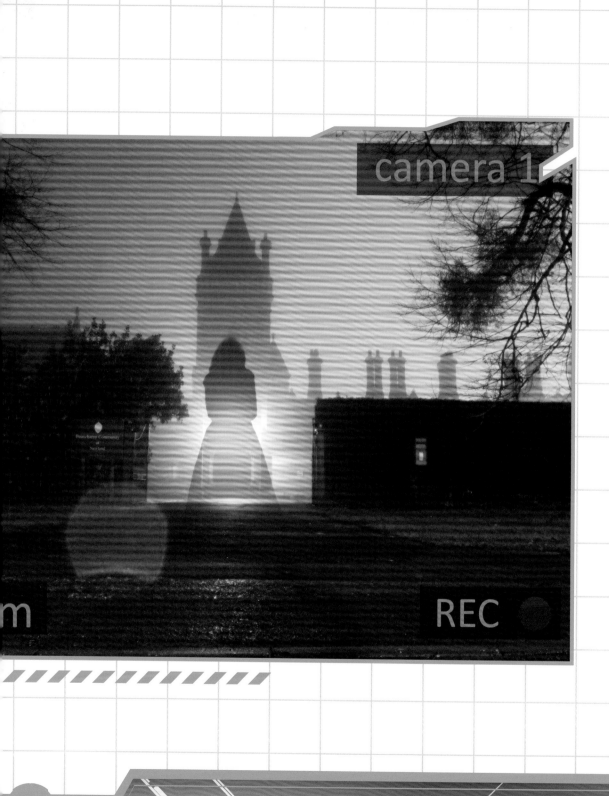

camera 1

REC

m

What do you think? Are ghosts real? Maybe. No one really knows. But with technology, ghost hunters are one step closer to finding out.

Glossary

app (AP)—a program that performs a certain task, usually on a phone

EVP (EE-VEE-PEE)—sounds or voices heard during electronic recordings that can't be explained; EVP stands for electronic voice phenomena

haunted (HAWN-ted)—having mysterious events happen often, possibly due to visits from ghosts

infrared (in-fruh-RED)—having to do with a type of light that is invisible to human eyes

joint (JOYNT)—a place where two bones meet

orb (OHRB)—a glowing ball of light that sometimes appears in photographs taken at reportedly haunted locations

page (PAYJ)—to get someone to come by repeatedly calling out their name, usually over a sound system

thermal (THUR-muhl)—having to do with heat

Read More

Andrus, Aubre. *Bloody Mary: Ghost of a Queen?* North Mankato, MN: Capstone, 2020.

Ransom, Candice F. *Eerie Haunted Houses*. Minneapolis: Lerner Publications, 2021.

Reed, Ellis M. *Ghost Hunting*. North Mankato, MN: Capstone, 2019.

Internet Sites

6 Spooky Things You Didn't Know About Ghosts
cbc.ca/kids/articles/monsters-101-all-about-ghosts

Are Ghosts Real?
kids.tpl.ca/wonders/682

Kids Ask! Can Scientists Study Ghosts?
sciencemadefun.net/blog/kids-ask-can-scientists-study-ghosts

Index

About the Author

Mae Respicio is a nonfiction writer and middle grade author whose books include *The House That Lou Built*, which won an Asian Pacific American Libraries Association honor award and was an NPR Best Book. Mae lives with her family in northern California. Visit her at maerespicio.com.